The body is where it all begins

THE BODY IS WHERE IT ALL BEGINS

Marcy Rae Henry

Querencia Press – Chicago IL

QUERENCIA PRESS

© Copyright 2025
Marcy Rae Henry

All Rights Reserved

No reproduction, copy or transmission of this publication may be made without written permission. No paragraph of this publication may be reproduced, copied, or transmitted save with the written permission of the author.

Any person who commits any unauthorized act in relation to this publication may be liable to criminal prosecution and civil claims for damages.

ISBN 979 8 3486 0174 7

www.querenciapress.com

First Published in 2025

Querencia Press, LLC
Chicago IL
Printed & Bound in the United States of America

ALSO BY MARCY RAE HENRY

dream life of night owls
we are primary colors

CONTENTS

the trouble in zazen 9

you could be the lake 11

my house seems unfamiliar 13

Saturday without a hangover 15

Prozac makes its debut 17

Fortuna wore a blindfold 18

consciousness seeks same 20

my boob popped out in the pool today 22

bailadora y boobs 23

shoes in mammography 24

despite the avoidance of red meat 28

She needs to know my skin isn't whitening but my hair is 31

Karnickelköttelkarnickel 36

Brancusi's birds above Breckenridge 40

(maybe Drăgaica) (maybe Sânzienele) 42

perceptual completion (how to fill in what is missing).. 43

real feel.. 46

unfinished/the Taos hum 48

begin by looking.. 50

Aaru (Field of Reeds) 53

maldiciones de odio y amor en los tiempos de mierda... 54

Acknowledgements 57

the trouble in zazen

isn't you, baby, it's me
i am embodied
fe-male formed
and appendages
susceptible to lunar phases
and feminine phrases
sorry, but no
no, but
sorry
perhaps it is my karma

some mahayana sutras
say women can be
    enlightened
only not if female
a woman about to reach it—
nirvana—
will be reborn
as a man

how many lifetimes
have i spent
    in the wrong body
in the right body
but not in the mood
earth moon and sun
are in constant relation
the way we aged
under sheets was terrifying
which way did you go?
i wasn't done looking

you could be the lake

places in my house
i want to take you

afternoon light beaming in the center
of prosecco rings on my dresser

palm prints on the headboard
moon pulling us inside out

the lake eats everything
not everything is digestible

you could be the lake
or you could be everything

something chest-level or top floor
or top shelf has me dumbstruck

water is a mystery
in all forms

you paused at my bookshelves
fingering orange spines

though not to scale, a tired map
contains the places we're from

you move like a day across the week
i'm drawn to blue around the world

we could go out tonight
or stand here forever under lights

planes flying in and out
flowers tangling

unless one of starts
the other can't let go

my house seems unfamiliar

        after a long trip
with no one to turn their keys
wind-up toys stop moving

someone taught me the difference
between wound (as in :
        : tightly)
and wound (as in :
        : painful)

when she reached for me in the car
        it got deep quickly
a blister engorges to protect itself

not all creation starts with pain or desire
(quiero querer means i want to want
        but could also mean *i want to love)*
some ventures need solitude

        in my house i am no longer waiting
when the sun peaks
a momentary glow before descent
saints don't come marching in but the ghosts

sitting on the windowsill
smoking redundantly into the rain
        because it looks good in a poem
my body still loud
and aging like the weekend

Saturday without a hangover

Slick as a tick it burrows in

The quickest way to clear it from the head is something a little stronger than the night before

But why have one when you can double the pleasure; when, after two, three is easy

After three you stop counting because they say it becomes 'bad for you'

And they mean all of you, from brain to breath to breasts

No two are alike, they say of breasts and snowflakes

Touch both of yours often, they advise, of what becomes a chore

Few chores rival cleaning up after the night before

To avoid embarrassment, throw away the evidence as soon as possible

Try not to count bottles, spills, splashes, or ring stains

Try to find the phone you hid from yourself

Spend a contrite week, a month, or forty-five days

Rest, and rest assured, the thought will return: I've been good, I deserve one, one more time

And, like that, slick as a tick, it burrows in

A song, a film, a smile, a slight, a glowing string of green and golden lights hanging in a window… any are enough to merit a toast

It may not take much to hang up a few Christmas bulbs, but to pull out a tick you must go slowly

Use tweezers, they advise, though I have used fingers

It's sly going in and sneaky about letting go

Make sure the head doesn't break off under the skin

The desire to be rid of it is overwhelming, and desire, of course, is capricious and impulsive

Suddenly, before you know it, you've pulled something out, you've opened something, popped the cork, pulled the tab

And once again, you will have to beat it, beat yourself; beat yourself up

Did you stay out of woods in Michigan, piles of leaves in the city, and bars everywhere

Did you avoid friends as well as forests

Friends mean well, but they may insist: just one, because we grew up together, because we had our first drink together, because we're one year older

If you manage to stay on track, any Saturday without a hangover is precarious

Don't step on a crack, don't call friends, reminisce or read too much

It's easy to give up, but if you can make it through the hour, the night doesn't seem so long

And don't make a big deal out of Sunday

Just remember to be grateful

Prozac makes its debut

On Sunday we agree it will be 1987 all day
even when we change the subject. A key
to a door that once opened to a garden.
The longing to pull the fire alarm. Driving home
a terrible parable. The record player moves
in a circle not a line. Lines on our faces
are mistakes. Classical continuity when a jump
cut would do. Heart on the radio.
Bands are like racehorses. Some like big fat houses.
It is not recall. Not regret.
It is small zesty shavings. Dancing on toes
when the soles will do. When holding hands
meant something. Beautiful and insubstantial
as a crowning merengue. Everything behind us
is in front of us. A decade of sunrise.
We were all unknown. We practiced drums
to acid rain. Built Thursday as if failing a test.
All day we believe aliens might save us.
We wait for 87 to kick in, for something
to restore our interest in daily living.

Fortuna wore a blindfold

tarot cards and tea leaves
superimpose faith over inevitability

twice a year the terminator splits night
and day with a straight line

the first red leaf prepares us
for icebright nights

when you try to tell her about
your trip to the Great Wall

she says she'd rather
see it from the moon

at the end of decomposition
humus increases the fertility of soil

everything is up for human consumption

what's tea is that everything leaves
even sun even moon

no need to pull a card

i know how it'll go
because i've done things to my heart

consciousness seeks same

        —after H.G. Wells' *The Island of Dr. Moreau*

     sculpting is to add or subtract
is it easier to doctor beasts out of men
     or make men out of torture?
the body is where it all begins
     he divides us of ourselves
until it becomes impossible to recall which way we began
     'not all living skin is painful' he insists
but the mind, helmeted by bone,
     is inescapable and i need to be saved
come on, moreau! tell me of your god (invention or intervention) tell me why i can't walk on all fours
     or why i drank a sinful last night
while it rained like a telegraph typing out:
     i won't come back for you   ever
everything needed to evolve is found in the sea
     i can still taste it
the moment we emerged covered in sea foam
     we breathed in fear

                which can't be vivisected
        and desire
                which can't be grafted
      the body remains in the mind
we're told it calls for meat and makeup
        'i've never seen an animal think' he insists
but he doesn't know i've been considering living quietly
          without cracking my gum
                or swinging my axe
god has left us alone on the island
        doing impressions of humans
            having a bad day

my boob popped out in the pool today

so i very gently placed it in the water
and swam away without it
if it wanted to be free then so did i

i studied ballet as a child. i was always the shortest one in class. my teacher would get on his knees to dance with me. & to tease me. he's now running for mayor in my hometown. & i hope he wins. right when i was switching to pointe shoes, my boobs grew. i felt like i was going to tip over. timber! so i quit ballet. & switched to modern dance. & my boobs were more manageable.

shoes in mammography

mashed and masked
gowned from the neck down
they try not to look at each others chests—
the reason theyre together in a sterile room
with pastel art and fake plants
they sit as far apart as possible
so the boobs just next dont add to the tension
they text partners and parents
ask friends: *when was the last time you got the squish?*
reminding but secretly wanting to share
the scare or laugh at all the names and tit emojis
they wonder why dressing room cabinets dont lock
why they dont open them and find butterflies
in all their symmetry
they count shirts bras jackets hats keys
until finally an empty space
in the waiting room
they find the tv too loud to drown out the nerves
of those who do this every six months

and think of boobs on billboards in spain

while americans be trippin over breast feeding

amid plastic plant vibes they think of thyroid protectors

while the boobs get zapped

the butterfly gland isn't affected

in mammography they close their eyes

in the waiting room they flip through magazines

with glossy perfect-tits

sneak a peek around the room—

rose-petal one-size-fits-all preschool painting-smocks

—the way people sneak a peek outside mammography

while they wait they look at

dirty sandals

skater high tops

fake vegan leather

flip flops

crocs

different colored socks

open toe

painted toenails
ankle bracelets
so much
to guess
from looking at shoes
before being facesmashed against a machine
someone yanking the chest breasts
in directions theyve never been yanked
outside of mammography
as they hate-appreciate the machine
they think there has to be an easier way
to look at the tits in four dimensions
without holding the breath turning the hips
standing on tiptoes and keeping the chin up
so it doesnt come out in the pix
they think about density and weather in boobs
and nipples and white matter
what to do monthly and annually
they think of everything

nothing and the mammographer who has held
and pinched and pulled and seen their tits inside out
but they havent even seen her shoes

despite the avoidance of red meat

as big as the tip of a pencil they say
of the metal piece that'll sit in the tit

does anyone still use pencils
to document, equate, or approximate?

some breasts look cloudy on machines
markers help point the way through

when weather in breasts changes
metal markers stay the same

like tits they come in different shapes
to mark time if not the moment cells go rogue

each time a new one is inserted we photograph
a love letter to the mammaries: just in case

to live is to be encased
you say: like sausage or offal

you know i hate the word 'offal' and wished
to go my whole life without writing about it

as condemned criminals were led off to cells
mobs used to throw offal at them

what would you like for your last meal? they're
asked to assuage the executioner's guilt

like most mugshots, there are no smiles
in the pictures we take

no visible guilt over what was eaten, sipped
or smoked, only scars

i tell you *being vegetarian is a way of life*
avoiding alcohol is just plain hard

you ask: how many pictures will we take
before it's time to give up the bra

as big as a sesame seed i say of the tiny
titanium clip replacing a nebulous tissue snip

She needs to know my skin isn't whitening but my hair is

It scares me to have my lists taken away

                                                             Wax
                                                             Stamps
                                                              Parchment

When I stay awake in the blackness
squinting myopically on my side of the border
I challenge myself to write letters to Z
and seal them in envelopes before I regret them

                      wolves cooperate on the kill
                      they can follow a scent across
                      the Río Grande

In the letters I ask her to bring me things I need in the desert
and draw crude maps where the road forks in my direction
    but I don't ask when she will return

Thread

Turmeric

Tulips

She needs to know I am brown but not embarrassed

I am naked at least twice each day   I just have to remind myself

  to stop dying

        in the feminine way   and to buy more things

                Whetstone

                     Oil

                Lemons

                Linen

While the wax is drying I write different endings to our story

        They always include the ceremony she suggested

          where we lick bee syrup off each other's fingers

And just when I make progress
    I erase and start over   (pressing on the pencil
      so the indentations will still be available)

                in a wolfpack
                only the dominant
                male and female breed

No question who would be top dog were Z and I wolves
She is monotheistic   foreign but exotic
  So she can come and go as she pleases

At times it pleases her not to respond
    Or to ignore my need for

    Matches
    Kindling
    Kissing

When she lived with me she'd wake at halfday and walk through
the living room halfnaked   her tips poking at her t-shirt
       implying flight   at any moment

    Sometimes she would bring me sunflowers
More than once she tossed my enumerations into a bin
       with ground coffee and piles of peels and rinds

   The victors gave us a saint and a prayer for lost things
        Hard to say if she is lost   or just gone
But if they keep bringing us old world diseases wrapped in blankets
  and plastic and setting the dogs on us   I'll have to keep
   shifting south and she might never find me

          even a lone wolf seeks out another wolf
          because wolves want
          to belong to each other

If Z comes back she'll have to be transparent
     as a palimpsest   and stop washing me off her
Then we can update the guest list
     and buy things to hold a ritual

                                     Censer
                                     Silver rings
                                     Hair dye

Karnickelköttelkarnickel

The first time the rabbit and I got a good look at each other in Lilian's apartment, we both scampered away, scared.

The rabbit had dark-grey fur and big, blank eyes. Lilian named it Gretchen. Then she took a trip to L.A. When she returned, Gretchen's balls had dropped.

Unable to hump the way his kind did in the wild, Gretchen slammed his stuffed animals. They'd slide around the hardwood floors and I caught Lilian holding them in place to 'help him out.'

Gretchen used a litterbox, but poops would inadvertently slip out and collect in corners like Cocoa Puffs. When I said it wasn't so bad because he only ate hay and vegetables, Lilian started bringing him to my place.

Rabbits' teeth continue to grow and they chew to file them down. Wood, paper, cables… everything but stone, which would do the job quickly.

Gretchen didn't play fetch or tug o' war, but I got used to him, even if he gnawed everything on my bottom bookshelves and his eyes reminded me of plastic.

The ex and I had just finished playing one-for-me one-for-you. We'd planned to marry then visit Iceland. I got the cuckoo clock, the telescope, and a box of her winter clothes.

When Lilian suggested she and I make the trip together, I bought her a glossy travel book. She said she liked to read them while boyfriends attempted to pleasure her.

We flew into Reykjavik around the Summer Solstice. Glossy fjords and houses painted like Easter. The midnight sun stayed in the sky the way a flag stays on the moon.

We shivered, back to back, dreaming of coffee. I wore one of the ex's sweaters. Lilian bought a thick scratchy one.

We got postcards of Dieter Roth's *Karnickelköttelkarnickel*, a chocolate Easter-Bunny-looking lagomorph made of rabbit poop.

The earth looked like the moon. The grey side of the highway bubbled and geysers erupted. *Geyser* comes from the Icelandic verb *geysa,* 'to gush.'

Lilian kept grabbing my hand, 'Let's go to Mexico. Let's go to Paris.' In the evening she said, 'Let's go to bed early.'

'Iceland,' I'd say while I slipped out alone to drink strong beer with kind strangers. And to talk about my ex.

A small cottage by the sea provided a pit stop. It had an oily roll top desk, an ancient organ that didn't work and wooden beds built into wooden walls.

I imagined the ex at the desk, making sketches of the sea. We would have made a game guessing which song the creaky instrument last played into the quietude.

Lilian didn't like isolation. She preferred minimalism and metal to wood. Maybe because of the rabbit.

As soon as we landed in Chicago, we stripped off a layer of clothing then went to fetch Gretchen at the exotic animals place in a small strip mall with a liquor store and a taquería.

The former attested: 'Before being boarded, Bearded Dragons are tested for Adenovirus, also known as star-gazing disease.' It sounded like a better way for a dragon to die.

Lilian was gazing forward. Thai on Tuesday, films on Sunday. Sex on Thursday? For Valentine's Day she bought me an electric toothbrush.

She made popcorn over the stove. Smells of hyacinths floated through open windows. While white kernels popped in yellow oil, I watched Gretchen hump his surrogates.

I didn't know how to tell Lilian the ex had contacted me. Wanted to visit. Lilian turned off the lights and started a movie. I placed rabbit ears among the other shadows on the wall.

Brancusi's birds above Breckenridge

Expanding   and   contracting

I haven't been here since I lost my virginity
We watched *Full Metal Jacket* afterwards
He fell asleep after the first climactic moment

In the cabin a book by a too-soft bed
Perimenopause is process not illness
    Women need 1-1.5 hours more sleep at night

Contract is agreement
The moment we contract disease
Something in the body agrees

I bend down to touch the river
I've spent 6,000 days of my life asleep
My body going on without me

Birds above open like artichokes
Head reduced to beak
A wing in flight

Years after the film I uncover the title's meaning:
A bullet with a soft core
Encased in hard metal

Holding their trajectory
The bullets have greater penetration
Against soft tissue

As the sun sets Breckenridge blues
I pick wild irises and put them in a room
Where no one will see them dying but me

if anger is a brief madness
the period is a week long
    being
        is the opposite of was
~~but~~ the opposite of something
made opposite again
is not the original
& neither am i
but i had a bf who told me:
there is a tradition in romania
where just for one night
you can be anything you want
maybe he said do anything
you want
& for one night we did
maybe we tried
what are we in the absence
of what we desire
maybe a brief madness
i've asked every romanian i meet
& no one has heard of it
but i'll keep asking
so i can believe

perceptual completion (how to fill in what is missing)

three:thirty a.m. rain patters the window kaleidoscopically.
late night becomes early morning.
last visit to Walgreens, shelves empty of sleeping pills.
the Brit said Victorians slept biphasically until the industrial age
and if empty American shelves weren't oxymoronic then what was.

cuatro:y media de la mañana. ¿cómo se llama *la Reina de Salsa?*
La Guarachera de Cuba que cantó 'si en mis sueños te di el alma mía…'
¿porqué no me puedo recordar?   perimenopause… dementia…
the American 2020 Trifecta?

los mexica didn't believe in el alma but in la memoria.
they made offerings of perritos, chiquitos
    placed hearts in a bowl
        bloody, beating offerings to gods of rain

                          ***

March 8: the last time we all went out. *twisted hippo*.
we ate off each other's plates, tasted each other's drinks.

March 16: a ravaged mercado. dry foods, frozen fruit, packets of vegetable soup.
a guy in an army jacket screaming he *had it*. clearing the aisles, loading his cart.

June 16: friends drop off wipes, port, forty pounds of dog food. les dejo frijoles
y calabaza con chile y tomate, comida de los Azteca, en la puerta.

August 25: in the dream world Ray and i rush to get to O'Hare. a back porch
filled with shoes. none with pairs. i grab yellow low tops, one bigger than the other.
the porch splinters, a dream into a dream. floorboards plummet behind us.
we can make it, i know we can.

***

i wake hot and humid. Celia's nombre como una canción en la cabeza.
when ovulation stops the period should act like punctuation.
pero el cuerpo no es un carnaval. it's a wait in line for the fun house.

> the dog leads me through a wet-heavy morning.
> children took chunks of chalk to the sidewalk to proclaim
> *we're gonna be ok!* rain erases vowels and consonants.
> the kids will come out later to fill them.

real feel

the real feel in chicago is 109
it is the experience of heat
makes me temper myself around you

my father used to run a beer mug under
the faucet before sticking it in the freezer
the first touch on frost left fingerprints

you are like the first night
sleeping in a new room
every time i see you
        one of us is taller than the other

after college i lived in a spanish attic
and two places in india without refrigeration

my father was the type of guy
who would say: *he's the type of guy*
who'd complain if his ice was cold

we're all abstract in the dark
a mosaic of yellow tiles floating out like bees
        almost a dead cow in water

i want to practice with you but it's no use
if i were a percentage i'd be halfway charged

in its solid state water can be held in the hand
but the experience of you lacks the real feel of you
if drained of blood the heart appears white

unfinished/the Taos hum

when orange has been
smashed to shit
pulverized to sticky
pummeled so much it turns yellow—
that is the color, my synesthetic friend says.

have you ever heard the Taos hum?
i ask. *it could be aliens or mind
control. it could drive you mad.*

someone whispers, *it looks unfinished…*
in front of an Agnes Martin painting,
like an embarrassed public prayer.
cloudy blue barely distinguishable
from white.

you wouldn't remember it.
you probably didn't notice how,

like Martin's lines, we almost touched,
almost became visible to each other.

not everyone hears 'the hum.'
some are hearers and some are listeners.
my friend said he could make a portrait of us
looking as if 'little work was put in.'

begin by looking

and because i feel gutted like a fish free of bones
no longer knitted together by skin and scale

and because the most peaceful i ever felt was living alone
in a monk's hut in the middle of India with panthers crawling
through early morning light as the sun cleared the mountain of guilt

and because i can't seem to reach you with brown fingers
snaked with veins undeniably full of themselves

and because it's not the right time of night or i don't have the right
rhyme or shyness gets stuck in the throat like a bone

and because ceroid cacti only bloom once a year for just one night

and because all the words i owe you are stacked like books,
like boxes, blocks and cans of food

and because you remind me of an earth held together
by magic and magnetic poles

and because you never get stage fright while i'm waiting
for the curtain to go up and a spotlight to cover us in shine

and because i got robbed on a train traveling through India
but still ride trains all the time

and because a fire in the fall smells as perfect as petrichor

and because some of my belongings were stolen at a Buddhist center
in Burma where i took vows of no killing no stealing no lying no
sexual conduct and knew there was so much i could do without

and because the antidote for feeling gutted is feeling grateful

and because in India i ate anything fried and soaking in syrup
i can imagine thighs in the game of cause and effect

and because no flag exists that would explain how i feel

and because only when i die can i say i had the time of my life

i could have made it
would've just made it
thru the buzzing field of reeds
into the afterlife
had i not
chased tumble weeds
& stopped to wash my whole body
as if it were a hand
if only i had entered
the right room on my left foot
before my heart was handed
to Osiris to be weighed
like one green apple
maybe if i hadn't become
accustomed to auditoriums
with acoustics as good
as my skull
hadn't drug tested
each stale month
earth-buried the dead
noted the day's time
& the sun
i would have noticed my heart
was being consumed

maldiciones de odio y amor en los tiempos de mierda

i'm writing her a poem about an alchemical tale
        i was told in Egypt a scarab pushes
bolitas de mierda down the road
        shitballs grow
                the way snow sticks to snow
when the beetle has dealt with enough shit
        midas-colored flies emerge and flit
              away forgetting where they came from
to ward off maldiciones   i'll give her a blue-green scarab
        that sat in my pocket while my body
floated in the Dead Sea   the way a sprig floats in oil

        ***

cuando era joven   people in charge talked
        about una llamada de dios
            and i'd lie on my side
as coyotes circled closer to the moonbright barrier
        between sagebrush and asphalt
            noting i had not been called

one nochebuena the first man   flipped me   upside down
        while tree lights glowed like planets
he pounded on my back   until   a peppermint candy
        lodged in my throat popped out
              and then the night was good

            ***

        pain is personal
            the weight of loving
                and being beloved
        the way brujería is more personal than soap
        amulets and sage
repetition is what keeps us together
            pero ella no se nota
        i've always had something stuck in my throat

Acknowledgements

Muchas gracias to my extended poetry community, including everyone at *Rhino* and *Querencia*. Thanks also to the following presses for publishing earlier versions of these pieces:

bailadora y boobs appears in **Cauldron Anthology**
begin by looking appears in **The Dewdrop**
Brancusi's birds above Breckenridge appears in **Panoplyzine**
consciousness seeks same appears in **Mud Season Review**
despite the avoidance of red meat appears in **carte blanche**
Karnickelköttelkarnickel appears in **Sundog Lit**
maldiciones de odio y amor en los tiempos de mierda appears in **Cathexis Northwest** and **DoubleCross Press**
my boob popped out in the pool today appears in **Pretty Owl Poetry**
my house seems unfamiliar appears in **Hags on Fire** and **Rogue Agent**
perceptual completion (how to fill in what is missing) appears in **Oyster River Pages**
Prozac makes its debut appears in **The Shore**
real feel 109 appears in **Mud Season Review**
Saturday without a hangover appears in **Rogue Agent**
She needs to know my skin isn't whitening but my hair is appears in **epiphany** and **DoubleCross Press**
you could be the lake appears in **Sunspot Lit**